How to Create a Successful Marketing Plan

Chris Lutz

Copyright © 2015 Lutz

All rights reserved.

ISBN: 151515002X

ISBN-13: 978-1515150022

DEDICATION

I dedicate this book to my Mom and Dad. If it wasn't for the support and start in life, I wouldn't be who or where I am today.

CONTENTS

Introduction
The Why
Reason for Having a Marketing Plan
Components
Mission Statement
Executive Summary
Competition
Implementation Strategies
Size Matters
Development
Involvement
Sharing and Editing Your Marketing Plan
Researching Your Market
Primary Research
Direct Mailing
Phone Surveys
Personal Interviews
Costs
Creating Your Market Plan
Preparing to Write the Marketing Plan
Financial Reports
Opportunities and Threats
Addressing Problems
Procedures
Marketing Objectives
Sales and Finance
Budget
Tracking Effectiveness
Conclusion
Marketing Plan Worksheet

ACKNOWLEDGMENTS

I'd like to acknowledge all the hard work entrepreneurs are doing out there in the world. It's tiresome and, at times, not very glorious, but the world needs you. Keep it up.

INTRODUCTION

Marketing plans are an imperative part of starting any business. They are used as a blueprint for mapping out the manner in which you will be able to achieve your business goals. A marketing plan is not only necessary for new businesses, as it can be used to help existing programs incorporate the strengths their company currently enjoys in an effort to implement necessary changes or improvements. A marketing plan can be implemented for a new product or service in which case it is meant to pull together all of the needed elements for an effective marketing start. It is important to have a marketing plan so that you can determine where you are, where you are headed, and how you will get there. It is especially important to have a marketing plan so that you can submit it for things such as loan considerations. As a whole, you should see your marketing plan as a process for which you have a team whole goal is keeping it simple, developing a time-frame, providing feedback, implementing necessary revisions, and remaining consistent with the mission statement.

The Why

Reason for Having a Marketing Plan

Your marketing plan is a small subsidiary of your business plan. The business plan is responsible for spelling out what your business does and does not do as well as the ultimate business goals. It is more than merely marketing as it discusses your locations, financing, staffing, and strategic alliances. It also includes your vision. Overall, think of the business plan as the cornerstone for your business. For new marketing or business measures, you need to alter the business or marketing plan. Your business plan should encourage an environment where your marketing plan can grow, thus both should reflect well on one another.

Components

There are many components to a marketing plan. The first component is a mission statement. Following this should be an executive summary. After the executive summary should be an internal or external analysis. You should include objectives after this point, followed by marketing strategies. Once you have determined your marketing strategies you should identify your resources, an implementation plan, a marketing budget, and evaluation methods.

Mission Statement

The mission statement should contain a clear description of the organizational identity, for what the business is meant, as well as which results your organization seeks. The mission statement should do more than just describe who is a part of the organization. It should reflect upon the internal and external perception in a manner which is understood by all. The mission statement should speak to what drives the organization and how things are accomplished within the organization. Overall, the mission statement should be simple.

Executive Summary

The executive summary acts as an overview which is readable and concise and summarizes the main objectives of your marketing plan. The internal analysis provides the background of the company, the current states, future directions, current resources, as well as the strengths and weaknesses of the company. The external analysis includes the economy, the demographics, trends, competition, and target markets. As far as opportunities and threats are concerned, you should understand that the environment will produce both. You should estimate the probability therein based on severe to not severe, as well as likely to very unlikely.

The Executive Summary should be brief, a single page, and located at the front of the marketing plan. It should use short sentences, bullet points, as well as bullet points for the major issues. It should spell out what someone reading your marketing plan needs to know in order to make sense of it all. The summary should provide readers with a concise description of the upcoming plans for your company while also boiling down your main thoughts. Generally, this summary is written after the completion of the marketing plan.

Competition

You should also list who your competition is, what their products and/or services feature, their pricing, their packaging, and their promotion. You should list the strengths and weaknesses of your competitors and how you are different. The customers and target markets section should include the current and potential customers, the requirements of the customer as well as the market clusters. For the marketing strategies you should include the customers, target markets, programs, services, packaging, pricing, and promotion.

Implementation Strategies

The implementation strategies should

include the steps, responsibilities, deadlines, and budget. The marketing budget should include the advertising, media, direct mail, databases, printing, production, and possible mailing. When you are evaluating your market plan you need to understand your success measure, the completion of action dates, accomplishment of goals and strategies, the results, as well as new customers, repeat customers, the average size of your contracts, and revenue.

Size Matters

The size of your marketing plan is dependent upon the size of your company. If you run a small company, you can generally create a marketing plan that is no more than a handful of pages, whereas a large corporation might have a marketing plan that runs over one hundred pages. In either case, the marketing plan should be placed in a binder where it can be referred to at least quarterly, but hopefully monthly. A section can be placed in the marketing plan for monthly reports on things such as sales and manufacturing for the sake of tracking performance as you follow your outline. A marketing plan should cover the length of one year. This is because markets will evolve, people will change, customers will leave, as will people. It is helpful to include a section in your marketing plan that addresses two or four year segments. Whether or not you do this, the majority of your marketing plan should address the coming year.

Development

You should make sure that you have a couple of months to write the plan before finalizing and publishing it, even if the marketing plan is only a few pages in length. The development of the plan is the hardest part. Executing the plan will bring with it challenges, but the biggest challenge is deciding what your company should do in the market and how to do it. Generally a marketing plan will begin with the first of the year or with the opening of the fiscal year if they are not the same.

Involvement

Everyone in your company should see the marketing plan. There are many companies who like to keep their marketing plans secret because they are ashamed of them, or they think that the information contained therein provides them with a competitive advantage. However, marketing cannot be done without getting people involved. Whatever the size of your company might be, you need to ensure feedback from every aspect of your company including finance, personnel, supply, manufacturing, etc… Getting every facet of your company involved in the process is important for many reasons. Part of having a decentralized company is that you can seek decision making processes that facilitate every member of the organization, in an attempt to ensure that all members feel as though they are a part of the organization. By allowing every employee to contribute in some fashion or another, they all feel as though they are a better part of the organization and as such work harder to see projects to which they contributed through. Since our company is not facing a crisis, there is no need to employ centralized decision making.

Even with decisions such as an annual marketing plan, the company will have less risks associated with dispersing power evenly, which also contributes to lower management levels, communication strategies, and better office relations. Employees are more motivated to perform for the organization of which they are a part, since they know that by sharing their ideas they are improving the organization. They feel as though their actions can improve the inefficient aspects of the company without having to take any idea to the top, while all management levels are able to utilize their knowledge and experience in their respective divisions. Taking advantage of decision-making from all employees will created the opportunity for advanced creativity and a better division of labor. A decentralized management will allow your company to diversify aspects of the company which we might not have done otherwise. Managers can be encouraged to use their own teams and each team can be responsible for an individual aspect of the marketing plan or review of the marketing plan. There are also cross-functional teams that work within all divisions ensuring that all employees are performing tasks above menial, allowing them to continually be challenged and continually work with one another. By facilitating better communication your company will able to improve efficiency within departments that might otherwise have failed to communicate. Your divisions must continually be in sync with one another, also contributing to more efficient workplaces and staff members. Your top levels still maintain the overall say in major company decisions, but other smaller divisions and teams and management are responsible for their individual aspects, all of which combine to make a large and impressive organization from the bottom upward instead of from the top downward, trickling slowly until some parts reach the bottom levels. This is the best way to ensure great marketing and company involvement.

Sharing and Editing Your Marketing Plan

When you are attempting to involve everyone in your company in the editing process, you need to provide everyone with access to your marketing plan. Thanks to modern technology there are a handful of viable options in sharing the marketing plan in any stage, receiving feedback, and group editing of the marketing plan. There are online forums such as Google Documents where you can allow access as "view-only" to certain facets of the company, while others are allowed "edit" functions when viewing the document online. Another popular method for group viewing, sharing, and editing of marketing plans is Dropbox. Dropbox is a software program which lets you sync documents between computers, iPhones, Androids, and online. You can share them with other computers and then edit them on the web later. Dropbox is a great mechanism used to sync files between a main desktop and a laptop. You simply install it onto the computers or iPhones which you are using and then drag your files and drop them into the folders so that they are synced between computers. After you create a user account, you can log in and see all of the computers synced to your account. If you use the internet interface you can view any of the files which were synced online. Using it is really simple. You download the software, whichever version you want for your computer, and then you create the Dropbox file. You create your online account which links all of your connected computers. Then you simply click on the file you want to sync and drag them to the Dropbox file and drop them off.

They will then be synced to the other computers and online. There are some great pros to the Dropbox including the free 2GB you get. It also has a great web interface which makes it simple to upload your files and access them later. It is compatible with Windows, Mac, and Linux making it perfect for nearly any users. You can share files through Dropbox and it is simple to use. If you have an iPhone or an Android then you have a mobile application you can use too. However, you can't use it with a Blackberry and the mobile applications are really limited. The basic version is free, but if you want to upgrade to the Pro 50 or Pro 100 then it will cost you either per month or annually. Overall the Dropbox software is great for anyone who just needs to send basic files or for businesses to share files from different locations. Multiple people can submit changes at the same time, mirroring the Google documents application and an integration of cloud computing. If you create documents which aren't shared to public folders, you can simply invite someone to view it and collaborate.

Depending on the size of your company and the needs of the employees, you can find the right offer for your company for a moderately low price.

Researching Your Market

It is important to research your market so that you have relevant data to aid you in solving any marketing problems which your company might encounter. If your company is just starting up, then this is absolutely necessary. Thorough market surveys function as the cornerstone for any successful business. Without market research you cannot identify specific segments within your market nor can you identify which of your products and/or services separates you from your competition. Whether you use experimental methods, survey methods, observational methods, or historical methods, you will end up with two types of data. The first is primary data which is gathered by an outside source but compiled by you. The secondary data is compiled and organized by someone else. This is the most popular source of information generally reported by government agencies, businesses within the industry, or trade associations.

Primary Research

Primary research can be exploratory or specific. If the latter, it is meant to be open-ended so that you can define a specific problem. It will require detailed and unstructured interviews which include lengthy answers solicited from respondents. Specific research is broader and is meant to solve a problem identified by exploratory research. In this instance, the interviews are structured and very formal. Specific research is the more expensive of the two. If you plan to conduct primary research with your own resources, the first step is deciding how you plan to question your target group. You can do this through personal interview, telemarketing, or direct mail.

Direct Mailing

For direct mail, the best way to ensure you increase the rate of response is to do the following: **Make it short and sweet Address questionnaires to specific persons Address questionnaires to people interested in the respondent Limit the questionnaire to two pages Enclose a cover letter from your company explaining your needs Send a reminder two weeks after the questionnaire has been mailed with a self-addressed, postage-paid envelope.**

Response for direct mail is generally less than five percent.

Phone Surveys

Phone surveys can be cost-effective, particularly compared to direct mail, with a higher response rate. The cost is one third that of personal interviews whose response rate rests around ten percent. If you choose to conduct market research via phone surveys ensure that:

- The interviewer confirms the name of the respondent at the beginning
- Pauses are avoided so that interest does not drop
- A follow-up call is made if any further information is required
- Interviews do not divulge details pertaining to the poll until the respondent has been reached

The typical rate associated with phone interviews is five or six per hour per interviewer. The best part about phone surveys is that you can cover a wide geographic with a relatively inexpensive rate, particularly since phone rates are less during certain hours.

Personal Interviews

With personal interviews, you will find two types. The first is the group survey while the second is the depth interview. The group survey is generally reserved for big businesses when they are brainstorming product modifications or new ideas as the results of group surveys can dictate buying preferences as well as purchasing decisions made by particular populations. The depth interview is a one-on-one interview wherein the interviewer works with a small checklist. These interviews can be focused or non-directive. Focused interviews include a pre-set checklist. With a non-directive depth interview, the interviewers encourage the respondents to discuss particular topics but with very little questioning. This design encourages the respondent to lead the interview.

Costs

When you consider which surveys should be used you should bear in mind the costs attached to each. For mailing, the costs are contained in the printing, envelopes, postage, cover letters, as well as researcher time, incentives, and time for analysis and presentation. For telephone surveys you must consider the costs for the interviewer's fees, phone charges, the cost of preparing the questionnaire, the researcher time, as well as the cost for the analysis and preparation of results.

Personal interviews incur expenses based on printing costs, cards if they are necessary, incentives, interviewer's fees, researcher time, as well as the cost for analysis and presentation. Group discussions will cost you based on interviewer's fees, recruiting expenses, rent for a conference room or another facility, researcher time, incentives, recording media, and the final analysis and presentation.

Creating Your Market Plan

No matter how you organize your marketing plan, it should be easily understood by all. You want to ensure that everyone in your company has access to the document both physically and linguistically.

Preparing to Write the Marketing Plan

There is vital information which your company should have gathered prior to writing the marketing plan. If you have everything that you need before you sit down to write, you will be able to avoid interrupting the writing process and thinking process. The first thing you should have when preparing to write the marketing plan is:

Financial reports

These should be profit and loss, operating budget, as well as recent sales figures relating to each product and region for the current year as well as the past three years. If your company is new, then you should have financial reports for as long as your company has been in business, or estimated reports. The next thing you should have is: **List of each product or service This should include everything in your current line as well as your target markets. The third thing you**

should have when you are preparing to write your marketing plan is: An organization table This is especially for the larger companies. If your company has less than five employees then you won't need this section. After this you should include: **Your understanding of the current marketplace.**

This includes a list of your geographic boundaries, your competitors, the customers to whom you sell, any distribution channels that you already have, demographic data, as well as information pertaining to trends in your current markets either product related or demographic related. It would be prudent to ask any of the employees currently in customer relations or sales to list the major points that should be included in the coming marketing plan. It is not necessary to include every crucial point, but taking a few into account is nice. Chapter Fourteen: Market Situation The term "market situation" refers to the best description of the current state of your current marketplace. This section should include the following answers:

- What are your current products or services?
- What are your current product lines or service lines?
- What is the dollar size of your current market or your markets?
- What is your sales set up?

- What is your distribution set up?
- To what geographic area do you sell?
- What is the population of your audience?
- What are the demographics of your audience?
- What are the income levels of your audience?
- What competitors do you have in this marketplace?
- How well have your products sold historically?

A market situation section in your marketing plan might look like the following: Markus and Associates is a legal firm started in 1988. We provide legal services to individuals and to businesses under $700,000 in annual sales. We provide legal support to those same businesses. Our market area is Jacksonville, Florida, and its western suburbs. For the personal market, our clients typically are in the $85,000 and higher income range, or they are retired with assets of $250,000 or more. For the business market, most of our work is for independent convenience store. With the exception of a poor period from 1991 through 1993, Markus and Associates has grown steadily from its creation. Gross sales in 1998 were $165,000. Competition for our immediate market is a group of six firms roughly comparable to our company. Only one of these firms, McCormick Legal, has an interest in marketing itself. We believe we rank third in the group of competitors, behind McCormick. We have a strong position in the convenience store portion of our business.

Generally, the head management team will have this information, but now you must write it down. The marketing plan is where you can pull all relevant information together and justify your actions for the following year. In the marketing plan you should consider how each of your services or each of your products compares to the services and products of your competition. You should explore whether there are opportunities within the market that neither you nor your competition is exploring currently. Also, while preparing to write the marketing plan you will discover that different members of your company will have different ideas about the current situation and the elements therein. You can use this opportunity to compare different aspects of the market against one another.

Opportunities and Threats

There are always good and bad implications within the current market. You should consider the following questions when determining opportunities and threats in the current market:

- Which trends in the market are working against you?
- Are there threatening competitive trends?

- Are your current products prepared for success in the current market as they exist right now?
- Which marketplace trends are working in your favor?
- Which competitive trends are working in your favor?
- Are your current market place demographics working for or against you?

You can locate this information from all over. You can begin with the city and state business publications, you can talk with local business reporters, you can browse chambers of commerce publications. You can also contact various manufacturers, read trade journals, or talk to the professionals within your association. If your company is simply creating a marketing plan for the coming year, it is important to address issues which were met during the last year in an effort to create and implement strategies to overcome them at present. Consider the following scenario from the previous year:

In a recent project (source: Project Connections, 2010), a company had contracted with an outside software developer (vendor) to provide software code (software program) that would be used daily by customers. On that first main project with the vendor, problems were encountered due to fast-moving schedules, early misunderstandings on requirements, management changes in the middle, and some unreliable performance to deadlines. As the team approached time to release the code for final QA prior to release, the functionality of the system they delivered was not all that we had wanted or needed. But time was short and the company moved into testing this first release. The outside developer was of course needed to support the in-house software team during testing, with fast turnaround on any remaining bugs.

Unfortunately, the issues and difficulties working together on the first development cycle had already created a strained relationship. By the time the teams were ready for Validation testing (an important step in software development to see that it works), the team environment was rife with tension, some finger-pointing and scape-goating, and general unpleasantness. In this difficult environment came the discovery, during QA testing, of a software bug that would cause horrible problems in certain customer usage scenarios. The software code in question was scheduled for its first deployment and customer use in just one month. An internal memo describing this state of affairs was circulated, and a low, rumbling panic began in the technical corners of the company. Political considerations kept the project in limbo for another two weeks after the memo was published. Meetings with the vendor's high-level management finally resulted in the assembly of an augmented project team to tackle the problem fast. By then, the teams had 12 days to design, complete, test, and implement the needed software code changes. Never had a deadline loomed so large or seemed so unreachable. It is important that the company be able to state the problems that have occurred, determine how the company could have avoided them, give guidance to the project manager of this project on how project planning could have been done.

Also, make recommendations for future projects of this type regarding the project life cycle, stakeholder management and creating effective project teams, and then determine what were the risks in this project and how could they have been avoided, as well as what were the shortcomings in the project manager's work and how could they be avoided in the future. The problems which occurred started with the fact that there were fast-moving schedules, adherence to which was either not done or could not be done. There were misunderstandings between the company and the outside software developer about the requirements. During the middle of the project there were changes to the management. For some deadlines were there unreliable performances. The functionality of the delivered system was not up to par upon the release time. It was not what the company wanted or needed. This presented further problems because there was limited time and the company had to adhere to the deadline for the testing for the first release.

Because the outside developer was still a necessary component for the testing, they needed to be there for the in-house software team during the testing period. There was a fast turnaround time to remove any remaining bugs, which placed an additional strain. Because of the aforementioned issues and difficulties between the company and outside software team during the first development cycle there was a strained relationship. The next time period was the validation testing which was an important step to determine whether or not the software development worked. With the tensions between the team environments, there existed finger-pointing and scape-goating, and general unpleasantness between the two. During the QA testing period, they discovered that a software bug existed which cause horrible problems in specific scenarios of customer could use.

The deployment of the software code was scheduled for one week from that date while customer use was scheduled for one month from that date causing panic among the already rift environment. After this, an internal memo circulated and all of the technical corners of the company began to panic. There were political considerations made regarding the project which took another two weeks of time after the date of the published memo. After this, meetings with the vendor's high-level management finally resulted in the assembly of an augmented project team to tackle the problem fast. However, by this point the teams had only 12 remaining days to design, complete, test, and implement the needed software code changes, a deadline which encompassed the most unreachable and large deadlines of the past. There are a myriad of things which could have been done to avoid these problems, each taken at different steps in the process. In the initial phases, given the fact that the schedules were fast-moving and resulting with people unable to meet them, this could have been a problem with a lack of understanding regarding the schedules, or the schedules literally being too tight. If the problem was the former then it could have been averted by speaking with every stakeholder and receiving written confirmation of their understanding of the deadlines and the requirements within those deadlines. If it was the latter, then more frequent communication between the company and the outside software designers would have been prudent so that any hindrances in terms of deadlines could be met head-on. If, for example, the outside designers had an issue within the first three days, that issue could be presented to management from the company hiring them and they could re-evaluate their overall deadlines to ensure that the software was designed to meet their standards, even if the time needed was a bit longer.

If they could not accept additional time, then the possibility would arise of hiring another outside company before things got worse. Stating that there were misunderstandings about the requirements could have been solved by requiring both parties to sign confirmation of their understanding of the requirements so that they would not create conflicts from that later in the design process. Changing management in the middle of a project will create fundamental issues between the two parties because of the shift in communication styles. It would have been best to avoid this change altogether, but if it could not be avoided, then everyone should have met with the new management and redefined schedules and deadlines and requirements. If there were unreliable performances for any of the deadlines they should have at once been stopped. The unreliable performances should have been reviewed and changed, and all pending deadlines changed to accommodate the new changes. If this had been done then the additional problems of the functionality not meeting requirements upon release time could have been avoided. If, however, that point came, then the company should have gone back with the software developers and pointed out exactly where things were not acceptable and what changes needed to be made, then had the software company fix them before the release.

While the company had limited time and needed to adhere to the testing for the first release, it would have been more prudent to fix any impending issues before testing, no matter the cost incurred for delays. Since there was an additional strain created from the fast turnaround to remove any remaining bugs, the company would have maintained the outside developer because they were necessary, but added to them and the in-house software team if possible to ease the burden of the time constraints, assuming time constraints could not be altered. If measures had already been taken prior to now, then the strain between the two groups could have been averted. However, if not, then it would be prudent to remind both parties that blaming people was not going to get work done and that at this point, it was not a matter of who was at fault but rather, getting the issues fixed as quickly as possible. Team building exercises could be done to build better relations between both parties so that the work environment could be more conducive to work. Ensuring that little measures were taken to bring the members of each party back together would be the best way to do this. There could be group meetings wherein each side could discuss the biggest issues with the software and the other teams, and then they could work together to find solutions to all of the issues.

With the validation period, again, hopefully at this point the aforementioned issues could have been worked out, but assuming they were not and we arrived at this point with these problems, then it would be prudent do many things.

The first is to take the bug which was found and immediately gather both sides together to determine which steps would be needed by both sides to remove the bug. Also, how long it would take, and then each party would have to sign a written confirmation of their understanding of the issues and the time periods in which these issues needed to be resolved. Instead of simply circulating a memo, it would be more beneficial to bring everyone together in a meeting to have these discussions.

These meetings might have to involve conference calls if the software developers are far away, but otherwise, any political considerations to be made should be discussed with both parties so that everyone is aware of what is at stake, what needs to be done, what decisions are being considered, what help might be needed, and how long it will take. With the most unreachable deadline and the largest amount of remaining work, an augmented team would hopefully be adequate, but they should have also included the original team in the augmented team to create more hands working and a better relationship between all working parties. For future projects of this type the project life cycle should have been created with all involved parties in a round-table effort to ensure that everyone understood and was confident that deadlines could be met. The stakeholder management, for future projects of this type, should have better communication between them at all times and if any rift is beginning to form, everyone should be brought back together in a manner which relates everyone to the issues at hand, the larger project, and less focus on individuals and seclusion or taking side.

Creating effective project teams means generally the same thing, that everyone openly accepts and complete understanding of the project and what is expected of them and their teams and that the work environment be one in which they can alert management of their status' throughout the project cycle and re-evaluate the project cycle if time constraints are discovered. The issues with the project included poor communication, poor management, misunderstandings, personal conflicts, strained relationships, secret communication, poor time management, and fiscal constraints. All of these are also shortcomings of the project management. Poor communication could have been avoided by better management and better acts between parties to ensure communication. Without getting written confirmation and understanding of all project deadlines, then there is no way for the project workers to create positive work relationships at the start of the projects. This would alleviate the misunderstandings as well. As far as personal conflicts, this could have been avoided by better managed teams whose relationships would not reach the point of strain if communication were improved and all involved parties were able to openly discuss matters in group formats instead of via memos or secret communication by upper echelons of managements.

Poor time management could be rectified, again, with better communication and working environments, and overall, fiscal constraints were a major root of the issues with this project because without wanting or having the money to spend on extending due dates, undue pressure was placed upon all parties involved. With better communication and management of teams, an understanding of the fiscal constraints could have inadvertently explained to all parties why time extensions were not permitted.

Addressing Problems

It is important to recognize potential

problems in new marketing strategies so that they can be addressed in the future. Assume that a new domestic tourism operator specializing in surf holidays wishes to build an interactive web site that allows the customer to see in real time the weather, wind, surf and other data relating to their destination. As a new and bold initiative the operator wishes to tie in the price of the holiday with the weather situation. Better waves and better weather attract a higher price and vice versa. It is a new and potentially risky project and the owner of the business has asked you, a recent project management graduate, to assist him in planning for this project. For the marketing plan pertaining to this endeavor, it would be product to list the following:

A) List the risks associated with this project.

B) List the top ten steps you would undertake in delivering this project.

There are many risks associated with building an interactive web site that allows the customer to see in real time the weather, wind, surf and other data relating to their destination. There are many risks involved in this project. Because of the interactivity associated with the design of the website, there are many challenges that any interactive website would encounter. The website would need applications which are hosted within an environment controlled by a browser. With the site you can update and maintain the web applications such as the live-feed weather reports. Potential problems include having to develop specific browser-based technology which might prove a costly endeavor, offset by users paying a monthly fee instead of downloading the software linked to the web access.

You might have to hire a web programmer to write the web application to work with your internet operating system which would incur an additional cost. This can reduce the number of errors in the program, which will help attract more customers, but there can be security-related problems with the frameworks of the program. Not only would you have to develop an application that links any weather software with the web access, but you would need to take on the risk and costs of creating an interactive payment program, and an equation for linking costs with weather, an endeavor which would need to be constantly monitored. This web site would sacrifice basic usability and user experience for the interface and weather updates. The issue of standard compliance might arise. As with any website, the browser applications are reliant upon access to the application files. These files are located on remote services which are accessed via the internet. If their connection is interrupted, then they cannot use the application. There is the potential for a loss of flexibility since the web applications are not always an open source.

This means that users are generally dependent upon third-party servers which mean there are no options for customization. There can be privacy issues associated with the fact that any company can track the actions of the users. There can be unwanted costs associated new software and necessary alterations to functionality. The risks associated with tying in the price of the holiday with the weather situation are quite simply the potential for a loss of revenue because of uncontrollable events. There are also risks such as determining how much to charge for any given weather situation and the amount of additional measures one would need to include in determining this number. There are many different factors such as wind speed, direction, etc... This would require meticulous detail into the influential factors and the affects that each had on the overall price for the vacation spots. Also, another issue would be people who book their vacations at a set price based on weather and upon arrival the weather changes, changing the price with it. There would need to be stipulations for whether or not they can be charged more or less upon arrival based on the weather, or if their purchase is finalized based on the weather at the time they book their reservations.

As far as the top ten things I would do for this project, I would begin with the browser type, such as Java or JavaScript to make the applications possible for each of the clients. The website would need a familiar interface that combines things such as the specific weather application, audio, video, and keyboard access. I would establish general purpose techniques that allow things such as drag and drop. I would integrate client-side scripting so that the clients can enjoy the interactive experience of the live-feed and up to date weather information without consistently requiring the page reloading. You would have to break down the necessary applications into what are commonly referred to as "tiers". Each of these "tiers" would be assigned a specific role. You would recommend a three-tier application for this site with the first being presentation, the second being application, and the third being storage. The web browser is the presentation tier. Web content technology is used for the second tier.

This is where the updates and user interface are generated. Since this is a moderately complex application for the weather, the third tier would provide users the continual access to the data. Since this interface is meant for a business, you would need to devise a business strategy to use interconnect the new software with the web access. You would ensure that all new features were implemented on the original server which would negate the need to upgrade. You would integrate the server-side web procedures such as the ability for clients to search and email. You would ensure that the website has cross-platform compatibility so that it can be operated within any web browser window.

Procedures

Understanding what potential problems might be faced and how a company can go about ensuring that marketing plans are implemented is one important aspect to a successful marketing plan. Consider the following example: Your company wishes to obtain data from private companies regarding their economic activity. The project requires 100 firms to be interviewed. These are split into 3 categories. The project manager has a timeframe of 2 months and has 3 employees to deliver this project. The results need to be verified by a second government department before they are used. For this project, the stakeholders include the project owner, project management team, the three categories of businesses, the second government department as well as the end user of the data. For each step of the project, it would be necessary to document written understanding and agreement from all involved parties to ensure that there is no confusion amongst any group and that each stakeholder is well aware of their responsibilities and their due dates.

For the design, you would need to divide the one hundred firms into the three categories. After this point, you would establish three teams. In this case, it would be one employee per team since there are only three employees tasked for this assignment. They would have to designate a specific goal for the number of firms interviewed per day. This would help maintain a consistent quota. Given the fact that the project needs to be completed and verified by another company before the two month time period, it would be best to acquire the results to the one hundred interviews as quickly as possible.

Assuming each employee works five days per week, ensuring the completion of at least one interview per day would mean that the total interviews per employee would be finished in a matter of thirty three days which is a little over six weeks, leaving one and one half weeks for the final review. It would be more prudent to establish goals of 1 ½ to 2 interviews per day to ensure that the other government agency has time to review the interviews. You would manage the stakeholder interaction in the design stage by monitoring the division of the one hundred interviews and the establishment of the 3 employees per one set of interviews.

You would also ensure that the project owner was aware and that the other government organization was informed of the time period in which they could expect to receive the completed work. If they reported that they needed the work soon to review, then communication between the three employees would be needed to speed up the progress of the interviews. For the inception, the three employees would need to be monitored for progress in terms of the interviews. You would manage the stakeholder interaction in the inception stage by providing updates to the project owner as well as the second government organization. You would supply them as often as requested, whether daily, weekly, or bi-monthly. This would require maintaining updates from the project management team as to their progress during a designated time period so that the current information can be passed along to the project owner as well as the second government organization.

For the scope agreement, you would need to ensure that every organization as well as business was informed of the deadlines, the goals, the necessary progress reports, and the frequency for all of the aforementioned. You would manage the stakeholder interaction in the scope agreement stage by ensuring that each group was in agreement as to their necessary deadlines. This would mean that the project owner was aware of the official deadline, which businesses were divided into which category, which employee from the project management team was responsible for overseeing the interviews of their designated group of businesses, the daily goals of the interview progress, as well as the length of time needed and given to the second government organization to complete the final review. For the delivery, you would need to ensure that the throughout the two months each of the employees from the project management team were meeting their goals in terms of the amount of daily interviews, that they were establishing current updates which were to be passed along to the project owner as well as the second government organization. You would have to ensure that the project owner was receiving the necessary updates and that the second government organization was also kept informed as to the progress and when they would receive the total project with the one hundred interviews.

You would manage the stakeholder interaction in the delivery stage by checking on each of the three employees to determine that they are filling out any necessary updates and that they have met their goals, combined their total interviews, and submitted them to the second government organization. For the review, you would need to ensure that the second government organization received the interviews and reviewed them within their designated time frame, you would manage the stakeholder interaction in the review stage by conversing with the second government organization to get written confirmation that they received the document with the interview materials and that they were reviewing. For the completion, you would need to ensure that the completed project was submitted back to the project owner. You would manage the stakeholder interaction in the completion stage by verifying with written confirmation the sending and receiving of the completed document from the second government organization to the project owner. These are simple concepts, though the detail in implementing them from beginning to end is a necessary component to the marketing plan because without that attention to detail, all employees cannot contribute because they will not fully understand, nor will you be able to dictate the necessary roles each facet of the company plays.

Marketing Objectives

In a marketing objectives section of your marketing plan you should describe the future picture. This section should answers that objectives your company wishes to achieve over the course of the following year. You should include a narrative of what you intend to accomplish alongside the data to support the objectives. As an example you could start with the following: Strategic management has recently expanded to include the management of logistics. Within the maintenance of logistics, information technology has played a large role in productivity. Thanks to the complex developments involved in travel, shipping, global supply chains, and supplying businesses with materials, logisticians have been called to ensure that businesses like ours are able to offer services which get all of their clients where they need to be and when. From this point you should be able to work with each department of your company to determine how the group best feels about implementing new strategies for the coming year, what things worked previously, what advances have been made recently that would help to bolster numbers for the following year, as well as how strategic management would work with the marketing plan at hand.

With the widespread use of technology, the coordination between logistics management has been greatly affected. Processing and communication has been improved which in turn increases interdependencies between different organizations. Technology has created computer networks which provide coordination between large numbers of people with the ability to work together. Computing tools and information technology have created new collaboration in the form of electronic collaboration, aiding logistics management. The effective integration of information technology has built commitment into business management, making it one key factor in the success of effective management. Interpersonal computing has made organization processes less expensive and quicker. Real organizations can dramatically reduce the costs of their coordination as well as communication through new information technologies radically creating more flexible organizations.

Conducting business logistics management to its highest capacity has been a conflict for small and large corporations since their inception. Aiding this challenge, technology has proved an effective medium for over one hundred years. Electronic collaboration is debated to have rescued communication, projects, data-entry, processing, and the continual search for better production. However, the all-encompassing rescue is now generating skepticism regarding its impact on creativity, effectiveness, and quality. Given research from the past decade, it is debatable whether or not e-collaboration has been an aid or hindrance; still, the more important inquiry is finding the balance for small and large businesses between efficiency and produced quality generated by the advancement of these technologies. E-collaboration spaces intended for advanced methods of maintaining contact with fellow employees during the work day and creating instant communication, ability to view availability, and create conferences, generated Lotus Notes and Domino. These environments expanded from military to business to educational with the development of e-learning environments catered to class discussions, class projects, and rapid accessibility to documents and information through Blackboard and WebCT. Sharepoint, and Documentum Eroom are additional portals developed specifically for the sharing of documents. While these systems allowed correspondence and minimal documental transactions, they were expounded upon to create the web "made up of millions of platform-dependent web servers providing users access to static and dynamic content through platform-independent web browsers". Overall, this produced browser-based systems within the web as well as the earlier non-browser based systems of peer-to-peer and client-to-server systems. These innovative tools for e-collaboration were founded and distributed by key players such as Microsoft, IBM, and Groove Networks and sharply reduced the cost of traditional business collaboration. All of the aforementioned platforms and systems have been exercised by small and medium sized enterprises as well as corporations in their marketing plans for the benefits of product innovation and infrastructure management. Corporations have learned from trial and error, gambling with large up-front costs, and merely predicting which of these methods best suits their needs as the technology develops and their new marketing plans have been developed.

Corresponding via e-mail is the oldest of these technologies and still functions as the most accepted means of asynchronous collaboration for all sized businesses. E-mail provides the ability to create mailing lists for specific teams both nationwide and internationally.

It allows a means of better organization and communication with all employees. Building off of email offers online discussion boards used for those for whom email is not a sufficient means of grand communication and require more focused discussions. These discussions can take place in online forums allowing for better monitoring of project progression. Advanced security measures allow centralized management to reduce their list management and create levels of viewing, editing, and access for clients and employees involved in said projects and forums. The Bulletin board system within forums allows members to complete an online profile, descriptive of their interests, which other members may view for the purpose of discovering like-minded personnel. Another large forum used in most systems currently integrated into daily business is the use of instant messaging (IM). This expansion is the first step to leveraging ease, speed, and affordability in this market. Instant messaging is allotted through systems such as lotus notes, aiming to provide continual access to staff through synchronous collaboration.

This portal delivers instant gratification as one is able to instant message a colleague once viewing their availability—whether they are listed as available, busy, or offline—to clear up minor matters with ease. Integrating calendars allows business to better coordinate office functions and meetings as well as tracking documents, notifying group members of new documents, and changes to documents in progress. Implementing special features within e-collaboration technology produces multiple layers of correspondence such as video streaming within an instant message. Incorporating voice and picture into these communication types presents us with sophisticated conferencing. The conference styles included are phone conferencing, which can connect business communities with other members nationwide at the same time. Video conferencing allows others to view not only the people with whom they are speaking, but also any objects held in front of the camera such as diagrams or charts. Both types of conferencing are offered through the web, with Voice Over Technology (VOT) for video phones, or Skype as a means of video and written chat, as well as via electronic connection for phones. These measures exhibit a larger use of telecommunications and international clients.

Sales and Finance

Your sales and finance departments should be able to work hand in hand when it comes to developing the quantifiable goals and costs necessary to implement said goals.

For small business owners, it is common knowledge that sales and finance are hardly able to interconnect, making the relationship between the two impossible until now. Thanks to sharing data online and sharing communication, sales and finance departments and staff can come together to maintain the best credit for your company. Prior to now, these two were completely separate departments or areas. The two have had a difficult relationship in spite of their actions affecting the success of each other. Profit levels, business volumes, tracking progress are all components of finance while sales is directed toward closing deals and continuing to grow the customer base. Finance is often responsible for the imposition of aggressive targets in terms of business restrictions. As far as sales are concerned, these moves limit their creative revenue and add unnecessary complications to the sales process. More often than not, Sales has viewed Finance as only caring about closing business instead of accurately billing and recording. However, in order for companies to effectively maintain their transactions including a debit as well as a credit, they must have a relation with each other so that there are no errors in invoicing, poor customer services, and broken processes.

Until now, Finance was not as privy to the complexities of relationships with the customers upon which Sales focused. Sales departments were not pleased at spending months creating good relationships with clients, only to have that relationship tainted by receiving an incorrect invoice from Finance. Thanks to new technology such as cloud computing, these two are forming a relationship with great communication, immediate responses, and improved collaboration. Modern accounting has now been linked to modern business, forming a relationship between Finance and Sales. The two can now invoice effectively, improve customer services, better understand credit balances, and collect cash in a more time efficient manner. Prior to now, Sales was reliant upon a system for managing customer relationships while Finance relied on software for accounting. This older software was often stored in a back office because it required significant upkeep as well as infrastructure which led companies to continue working with systems which were a decade or two old. Thanks to cloud computing, accounting systems have grown and advanced to allow companies to work with the best software. This has encouraged a mind-set for Finance that is customer-centric, much to the appreciation of Sales. The customer relationship management systems have been integrated into the cloud along with accounting software which allows the two departments to inter-connect, share data up-to-the-minute and collaboration online.

This collaboration has allowed the Sales' revenue to grow thanks to new accounts, better customer service, an improved corporate reputation, and extra sales. In order to define future strategy, Sales requires a forecast from Finance which is often times convoluted at bust when reported. This forecast dictates the allocation of resources and time. Cloud computing has created the close communication between Finance and Sales which has allowed for more direct forecast reports. This has allowed for more accurate data to be exchanged between the two departments by maintaining accounting applications and customer relations management applications to work in sync. Answers regarding invoices can be provided immediately with cloud computing as opposed to the past when Sales would have to email Finance and would only respond to the customer once they had received a response.

Budget

Your marketing plan should include a section which allocates the necessary budgets for each anticipated activity that year. People in charge of each subsection of each new activity should be informed as to their allotted budget. The anticipated costs should be approached in an objective manner. If you have no budget experience, then you should add at least 25% to any estimate. You should also include a budget for internal hours and external costs. The budget should be maintained on a spreadsheet or in Lotus so that it can be manipulated throughout the process. Your budget section might include the following: Gross Sales $140,000 Budget for annual marketing $8,045 Yellow Pages$2,400 Sales letter mailing $600 Clerical help for mailing list$135 Advertising in local magazine $400 Advertising in local business newspaper $1,300 Brochure design plus copywriting $420 Brochure Printing $375 New mailing label software$250 Registration for business exhibition $125.

Tracking Effectiveness

In order to track the progress of your marketing plan as the year progresses, you should establish regular meetings. You should develop a plan for incorporating adjustments, a plan for monitoring sales progress, as well as a plan for monitoring costs. You should be able to state what was accomplished during the last quarter during each meeting, how much of the budget was spent, and what else is anticipated for the following quarter. At each meeting, reports should be verbal with a printed copy. Whatever changes you decide to implement as the year progresses, they should be included in the marketing plan.

Conclusion

The marketing plan should address the short term (which is one to twelve months) as well as the long term (which is over twelve months). It should outline the major goals of the year while also analyzing the mechanics necessary to meet those goals, bringing together the short term actions with the long term goals. It is good to think beyond the upcoming year and include the next few years in your planning. You should be able to anticipate how many employees you will add over the upcoming years, how much office space you will need, whether your staff should endure additional training or certification, if you will hire another manager, whether or not you will be purchasing major equipment, how you can improve your profit margins, how to become active in local trade groups, regional trade groups, or national trade groups, as well as how the market demographics will affect your business in the future. Overall, your marketing plan acts as the key ingredient to a successful business plan and business.

Marketing Plan Worksheet

In the absence of a fully written plan, a simple worksheet where you can clearly visualize your efforts, time frame, and other criteria can be just as powerful. I prefer to use this one below. We use these internally for many new individual projects, not just as a complete plan for a whole business.

(Complete one for each project, if you have more than one.)

Project 1:

Target Market Description: (size, demographics, buying characteristics, problems, etc)	
Marketing Strategy 1:	Key tasks: • • • • •
Marketing Strategy 2:	Key tasks: • • •
Marketing Strategy 3:	Key tasks: • • •

Marketing Strategy 4:	Key tasks: • • •
Marketing Strategy 5:	Key tasks: • • •
Marketing Strategy 6:	Key tasks: • • •
Marketing Strategy 7:	Key tasks: • • •

Action Plan

Initial Project Set Up Tasks	Deadline	Responsibility

Ongoing Tasks – Per Project	Deadline	Responsibility

Ongoing Business Tasks (overall business)	Deadline	Responsibility

Potential Obstacles

Obstacle	Resource/Solution	Where to Find It

Other Notes:

Profitability Analysis
(do estimates on separate spreadsheet, per month and year)

Project Profitability:
(complete for each project)

Total Estimated Expenses (total expenses for individual project)	
Total Estimated Revenue (total revenue for individual project)	
Total Estimated Profit (total revenue – total profit)	
Estimated Return on Investment (total profit/total expense)	

ABOUT THE AUTHOR

Chris Lutz is an American entrepreneur living in the mid-Atlantic on the East coast. He's always wanted to be an entrepreneur and turn his interests and passions into businesses. He'd like to connect and become friends with other entrepreneurs from all industries.

Chris is the founder and owner of S.P.A.R.T.A.

He holds a BS degree in Exercise Science from George Mason University.

Chris is the author of several other books that can be found on Amazon.

His business, www.theentrepreneurlifestyle.com is a celebration of the lifestyle of entrepreneurs, from struggle to success with eBooks, tools, training, and other resources for entrepreneurs.

www.ingramcontent.com/pod-product-compliance
Lightning Source LLC
Chambersburg PA
CBHW072309200526
45168CB00014B/1181